Next Level Living

WORKBOOK

Linda McLean

Includes BONUS 32 Day Gratitude Journal

Quantity discounts are available on bulk orders.
Contact info@TAGPublishers.com for more information.

TAG Publishing, LLC
2618 S. Lipscomb
Amarillo, TX 79109
www.TAGPublishers.com
Office (806) 373-0114
Fax (806) 373-4004
info@TAGPublishers.com

ISBN: 978-1-934606-36-0

First Edition

Contents

Your Journey Begins

Your Journey Continues...

Your Journey Begins

Congratulations on making a decision to take your life to the next level by purchasing this companion workbook to **Next Level Living: Today's Guide for Tomorrow's Abundant Life**! You now have a complete package that will help you move in the direction of your goals with more precision and purposeful planning than ever before.

As you read the book, using this workbook provides you with the perfect place to complete your exercises, capture your daily gratitude lists, and record your thoughts, observations, daily reflections and enlightening "ah-ha" moments. Within this workbook, you will find that each day's activities coincide with the lessons taught in the book, making your journey flow naturally and with ease; all you need to do is fill in the blanks.

Your workbook will serve as an ongoing reference for the days, months and even years to come. How exciting and insightful it is to revisit your written goals from previous years, by that time you're either living life at a different level or very close to it. It is a true testament to how far you have come and what you have accomplished. It serves as a tool to reflect on and assess your personal journey for years to come!

Lastly, if you find yourself needing some additional support along the way, please let me know. There are **Next Level Living** webinars, teleseminars, telephone and in-person coaching sessions available to support you in your process of change and growth. Please visit www.NextLevelLivingbook.com for more information.

It is my pleasure to support you as you journey to the next level!

Linda

SECTION ONE:

Understand Your Marvelous Mind

Day 1 ◆ Decide to Do Something

Begin Each Day with Gratitude

10 things I am grateful for today…

1. _____
2. _____
3. _____
4. _____
5. _____
6. _____
7. _____
8. _____
9. _____
10. _____

Daily Action

Baed on what you have read so far in the book, what does "Next Level Living" mean to you?

_____
_____
_____
_____
_____
_____

_____

_____

_____

_____

_____

Daily Reflection

Before going to bed, review your gratitude list and reflect on the day's accomplishments. Many times we overlook what we have accomplished because we think it is trivial; but trivial to whom? Look for the good in what you did today. Embrace it and move forward.

_____

_____

_____

_____

_____

Now, picture the amazing day you will have tomorrow. The most powerful times to feed your subconscious mind are first thing in the morning and right before you go to sleep. Because when you drift off to sleep with peaceful, positive thoughts, you sleep better and your last thoughts sink deep into your subconscious. This subtly shifts your next day's actions in a way that helps create what you really want out of life.

Tomorrow is a new day, filled with new opportunities.

SECTION ONE ◆ Day 2

Day 2 ◆ Study Gratitude

Begin Each Day with Gratitude

10 things I am grateful for today…

1. _____

2. _____

3. _____

4. _____

5. _____

6. _____

7. _____

8. _____

9. _____

10. _____

Daily Action

Make a copy of today's gratitude list and carry it with you throughout the day reflecting on it often. Notice how dwelling on the things you are grateful for makes a difference. *(You could photocopy your list or transfer it to note cards, your smart phone, smart tablet or anything else you carry with you. Ideally, you could bring your Workbook with you to review throughout the day.)*

How are you going to keep your list in front of you today?

_____

_____

_____

_____

www.NextLevelLivingBook.com

Daily Reflection

Before going to bed tonight, review your gratitude list and reflect on the day's accomplishments. Take a moment to feel proud of the time you have invested so far in your journey to the next level. Look for the good in what you did today. Also look closely for any connections between your thoughts, actions, and results. They may not seem evident yet, but know and believe they are there, waiting to reveal themselves further along in your journey. For now, embrace your accomplishments and move forward.

_____

_____

_____

_____

_____

_____

_____

_____

_____

_____

As you close your eyes, visualize the amazing day you will have tomorrow.

Tomorrow is a new day, filled with new opportunities.

SECTION ONE ◆ Day 3

Day 3 ◆ Learn How to Learn

Begin Each Day with Gratitude

10 things I am grateful for today…

1. _____

2. _____

3. _____

4. _____

5. _____

6. _____

7. _____

8. _____

9. _____

10. _____

Daily Action

The realization is that we are getting certain results in our lives — some positive and some negative. What results are you seeing that you really LIKE? What results are you seeing that you really DON'T LIKE? Jot down a few that come to mind and then return to this list and add to it as you observe your life this week.

Results I LIKE:

1. _____

2. _____

3. _____

4. _____

www.NextLevelLivingBook.com

5. —————————————————————

6. —————————————————————

7. —————————————————————

Results I DON'T LIKE:

1. —————————————————————

2. —————————————————————

3. —————————————————————

4. —————————————————————

5. —————————————————————

6. —————————————————————

7. —————————————————————

Daily Reflection

I hope you enjoyed this peek behind the curtain of the inner workings of your mind. Being aware of the connection between your thoughts, images and emotions is critical to understanding your mind and making the changes you desire. Now, as you prepare to turn off your mind for some well deserved sleep, it's time to review your gratitude list and reflect on the day's accomplishments. Find the good in what you did today. Embrace it and move forward.

—————————————————————

—————————————————————

—————————————————————

As you close your eyes tonight, picture the amazing day you will have tomorrow.

Tomorrow is a new day, filled with new opportunities.

Day 4 ◆ Discover "Reality"

Begin Each Day with Gratitude

10 things I am grateful for today...

1. _____

2. _____

3. _____

4. _____

5. _____

6. _____

7. _____

8. _____

9. _____

10. _____

Daily Action

Looking at the list of results that you wrote down yesterday, consider those you LIKE and those you DON'T LIKE. What kind of thinking might be the cause of these results?

Results I LIKE	What kind of thinking might be the cause?

Results I Don't Like	What kind of thinking might be the cause?

Daily Reflection

Before going to bed, review your gratitude list and reflect on the day's accomplishments. Look for the good in what you did today. Embrace your accomplishments and the knowledge you gained today, and visualize yourself moving forward to the next level.

_____

_____

_____

_____

_____

_____

_____

As you close your eyes, picture the amazing day you will have tomorrow.

Tomorrow is a new day, filled with new opportunities.

Day 5 ◆ See How the Mind Matters

Begin Each Day with Gratitude

10 things I am grateful for today…

1. _____

2. _____

3. _____

4. _____

5. _____

6. _____

7. _____

8. _____

9. _____

10. _____

Daily Action

Today, write at least three Old Beliefs you have and then craft the New Beliefs you would like to replace them with. Here are some examples to get you thinking:

Old Beliefs	New Beliefs
Can't lose weight	*I am maintaining a healthy weight*
Can't cook	*I am easily creating a delicious meal*
Terrible with Money	*I am successfully working on my money management skills*

Old Beliefs	New Beliefs
_____	_____
_____	_____
_____	_____
_____	_____
_____	_____
_____	_____

Daily Reflection

Before going to bed, review the gratitude list that came from your heart this morning and reflect on your accomplishments and next level lessons learned today. Look for the good in your day, embrace it and move forward.

_____

_____

_____

_____

As you close your eyes, picture the amazing day you will have tomorrow.

Tomorrow is a new day, filled with new opportunities.

www.NextLevelLivingBook.com

Day 6 ◆ Identify Your Support Beams

Begin Each Day with Gratitude

*10 **individuals** I am grateful for today…*

1. _____
2. _____
3. _____
4. _____
5. _____
6. _____
7. _____
8. _____
9. _____
10. _____

Daily Action

What and who will keep me uplifted and motivated as I strive to make changes in my life? For examples please be sure and refer back to the Appendix section of the book.

My Support Beams:

1. _____ 2. _____
3. _____ 4. _____
5. _____ 6. _____
7. _____ 8. _____
9. _____ 10. _____

Daily Reflection

Before going to bed, review your list of people you are grateful for, your support beams list from today's action, and then reflect on the day's accomplishments. Look for the good in what you did today – what happened today that made you smile? Embrace that feeling and move forward.

_____

_____

_____

_____

_____

_____

_____

_____

_____

_____

_____

_____

_____

As you close your eyes, picture the amazing day you will have tomorrow.

Tomorrow is a new day, filled with new opportunities.

Day 7 ◆ Choose Who You Will Be

Begin Each Day with Gratitude

10 things I am grateful for today…

1. _____
2. _____
3. _____
4. _____
5. _____
6. _____
7. _____
8. _____
9. _____
10. _____

Daily Action

With an open, forgiving mind, write a list of Old Beliefs about yourself — the ones that have only limited you *(we talked about them on Day 5)*. Who gave you these Old Beliefs? Now in your own heart (or out loud), give those limitations back to the person who gave them to you.

What was an "Old Belief" I received?	And from Whom?
"I will never be good at writing poetry, and I should find something else to do."	*"My father."*

What was an "Old Belief" I received?	And from Whom?

Daily Reflection

Before going to bed, review your gratitude list and congratulate yourself on your accomplishments today. Look for the good in what you did today. Embrace the freedom and sense of lightness you feel from giving back your "old beliefs" and move forward with the new ones you've replaced them with.

_____

_____

_____

_____

_____

_____

_____

As you close your eyes, picture the amazing day you will have tomorrow.

Tomorrow is a new day, filled with new opportunities.

Day 8 ◆ Change without Blame

Begin Each Day with Gratitude

10 things I am grateful for today…

1. _____
2. _____
3. _____
4. _____
5. _____
6. _____
7. _____
8. _____
9. _____
10. _____

Daily Action

In looking at all the areas of your life (personal, work, spiritual, etc.) what do you want to:

◆ Redecorate: a kind of sprucing up, making changes that are mostly cosmetic to reflect changes in style or direction *(ex. apply new time management skills)*.

◆ Remodel: applies to circumstances that dictate more significant changes in the configuration of our lives without really having to take it down to the ground. This is when a moderate shift or change will produce the desired result *(ex. adjust daily activities now that children are in college)*.

◆ Rebuild: when we are faced with life altering situations, they often require life altering solutions *(ex. life after divorce)*.

Areas of my Life I want to REDECORATE and why:

1. _____
2. _____

Areas of my Life I want to REMODEL and why:

1. _____

2. _____

Areas of my Life I want to REBUILD and why:

1. _____

2. _____

Daily Reflection

Before going to bed, review your gratitude list and reflect on the day's accomplishments. Reflect on the good in what you did today and visualize moving toward your Next Level of Living. Embrace the feeling of forward momentum as you decide to redecorate, remodel or rebuild various areas of your life.

_____

_____

_____

_____

_____

_____

_____

_____

As you close your eyes, picture the amazing day you will have tomorrow.

Tomorrow is a new day, filled with new opportunities.

Day 9 ◆ Embrace Truth

Begin Each Day with Gratitude

10 things I am grateful for today…

1. _____

2. _____

3. _____

4. _____

5. _____

6. _____

7. _____

8. _____

9. _____

10. _____

Daily Action

Create your Ultimate Personal Dream List. This list includes who I want to BE, what I want to Do and what I want to HAVE.

Who I want to **BE** (or become) before I leave this earth:

1. _____

2. _____

3. _____

4. _____

5. _____

6. _____

7. _____

8. _____

9. _____

10. _____

11. _____

12. _____

13. _____

14. _____

15. _____

16. _____

17. _____

18. _____

19. _____

20. _____

21. _____

22. _____

23. _____

24. _____

25. _____

26. _____

27. _____

28. _____

29. _____

30. _____

What I want to **DO** before I leave this earth:

1. _____

2. _____

3. _____

4. _____

5. _____

6. _____

7. _____

8. _____

9. _____

10. _____

11. _____

12. _____

13. _____

14. _____

15. _____

16. _____

17. _____

18. _____

19. _____

20. _____

21. _____

22. _____

23. _____

24. _____

25. _____

26. _____

27. _____

28. _____

29. _____

30. _____

What I want to **HAVE** before I leave this earth:

1. _____

2. _____

3. _____

4. _____

5. _____

6. _____

7. _____

8. _____

9. _____

10. _____

11. _____

12. _____

13. _____

14. _____

15. _____

16. _____

17. _____

18. _____

19. _____

20. _____

21. _____

22. _____

23. _____

24. _____

25. _____

26. _____

27. _____

28. _____

29. _____

30. _____

Daily Reflection

Before going to sleep tonight and allowing your subconscious mind to dream as big as it wants to, review your gratitude list and reflect on the day's accomplishments. Look for the good in what you did today. Embrace all if it and move forward.

_____

_____

_____

_____

_____

_____

_____

_____

_____

_____

_____

_____

_____

_____

_____

_____

_____

_____

As you close your eyes, picture the amazing day you will have tomorrow.

Tomorrow is a new day, filled with new opportunities.

Day 10 ◆ Make Change Possible

Begin Each Day with Gratitude

*10 **habits** I am grateful for today…*

1. _____

2. _____

3. _____

4. _____

5. _____

6. _____

7. _____

8. _____

9. _____

10. _____

Daily Action

Which of your daily habits (where you wear your watch, the sock you usually put on first, how you start each morning, etc) would you be willing to change?

_____

For the next 10 days make the change in this habit and document what you learn from the whole process. This exercise is simply to prove to yourself that you can create change in your life.

_____

_____

_____

_____

_____

_____

Daily Reflection

Before going to bed, review your list of positive habits and reflect on how they contributed to the day's accomplishments. Celebrate the results you noticed today. Whether you consider the results big or small, they are all victories. Embrace the feeling of winning and move forward.

_____

_____

_____

_____

_____

_____

_____

_____

As you close your eyes, picture the amazing day you will have tomorrow.

Tomorrow is a new day, filled with new opportunities.

SECTION TWO:

Chart Your Course

Day 11 ◆ Find Out "What Is"

Begin Each Day with Gratitude

10 things I am grateful for today…

1. _____

2. _____

3. _____

4. _____

5. _____

6. _____

7. _____

8. _____

9. _____

10. _____

Daily Action

For this exercise, I will leave my emotions at the door and as objectively as possible write down "what is" in each of the eight areas of my life listed below. I will include those things that are good in my life as well as those I want to change.

"What is"…

…in the **Health** area of my life?

_____

_____

...in the **Relationship** area of my life?

_____

_____

...in the **Financial** area of my life?

_____

_____

...in the **Business/Career/Education** area of my life?

_____

_____

...in the **Spiritual** area of my life?

_____

_____

...in the **Recreational** area of my life?

_____

_____

...in the **Community** area of my life?

_____

_____

...in the **Personal Growth** area of my life?

_____

_____

Daily Reflection

Before going to bed tonight, review your gratitude list and reflect on the day's accomplishments. Look for the good in all areas of your life. Embrace the feeling of taking steps forward in your journey.

_____

_____

_____

_____

_____

_____

_____

_____

_____

_____

_____

_____

As you close your eyes, picture the amazing day you will have tomorrow.

Tomorrow is a new day, filled with new opportunities.

Day 12 ◆ See How You Got Here

Begin Each Day with Gratitude

10 things I am grateful for today…

1. _____

2. _____

3. _____

4. _____

5. _____

6. _____

7. _____

8. _____

9. _____

10. _____

Daily Action

These are the current influences in my life categorized by type of association.

1. Disassociations (where I need to end the relationship)
   Who?

   _____

   _____

2. Limited Associations (where I need to reduce time in the relationship)
   Who?

   _____

   _____

3. Expanded Associations (where I need to invest more time in the relationship)
   Who?

_____

_____

How can I mirror the success I see in each of the people on the Expanded Associations list?

_____

_____

_____

Daily Reflection

Before going to bed, reflect on your day's accomplishments. Bask in the positive effect they have had on your life. Embrace this feeling of happiness and warmth and visualize yourself moving forward toward your *Next Level of Living*.

_____

_____

_____

_____

_____

As you close your eyes, picture the amazing day you will have tomorrow.

Tomorrow is a new day, filled with new opportunities.

Day 13 ◆ Accept "What Is"

Begin Each Day with Gratitude

10 things I am grateful for today…

1. _____
2. _____
3. _____
4. _____
5. _____
6. _____
7. _____
8. _____
9. _____
10. _____

Daily Action

What are three things that you have a tendency to blame someone or something else for? Take a moment to think about how you might have blamed or perhaps are still blaming someone for your current situation.

Who Do I Blame?	What Do I Blame Them For?

Daily Reflection

Before going to bed, review your gratitude list and reflect on the day's accomplishments. See the good in what you did today. Embrace it and move forward.

_____

_____

_____

_____

_____

_____

_____

_____

_____

_____

_____

_____

_____

As you close your eyes, picture the amazing day you will have tomorrow.

Tomorrow is a new day, filled with new opportunities.

Day 14 ◆ Recognize that You Deserve a Great Life

Begin Each Day with Gratitude

10 things I am grateful for today…

1. _____

2. _____

3. _____

4. _____

5. _____

6. _____

7. _____

8. _____

9. _____

10. _____

Daily Action

What are the negative things you have been saying to yourself? Next, write out what POSITIVE "self-talk" you will replace those negative things with. POSITIVE "self-talk" is what will carry you forward.

The following are NEGATIVE things I have been saying to myself:

1. _____

2. _____

3. _____

4. _____

5. _____

I commit to replace those negative things with the following POSITIVE "self-talk":

1. _____

2. _____

3. _____

4. _____

5. _____

Daily Reflection

Before going to bed, review your gratitude list, particularly the positive things about yourself and how they have contributed to who you are today. Look for the good in what you did, thought and learned today. Embrace it all and move forward.

_____

_____

_____

_____

_____

_____

_____

_____

As you close your eyes, picture the amazing day you will have tomorrow.

Tomorrow is a new day, filled with new opportunities.

Day 15 ◆ Know Yourself and Others

Begin Each Day with Gratitude

10 things I am grateful for today…

1. _____

2. _____

3. _____

4. _____

5. _____

6. _____

7. _____

8. _____

9. _____

10. _____

Daily Action

Getting to know yourself better means being clear about your strengths and weaknesses. The key to growth is knowing how to develop your strengths and manage your weaknesses.

My three greatest strengths:

1. _____

2. _____

3. _____

What will I do to develop these strengths?

1. _____

2. _____

3. _____

My three greatest weaknesses:

1. _____

2. _____

3. _____

What will I do to manage these weaknesses?

1. _____

2. _____

3. _____

Daily Reflection

Before going to bed, review your gratitude list and reflect on the day's accomplishments and all the knowledge about understanding yourself and others that you have gained today. Look for the good in your thoughts, words, actions and results. Embrace it all and visualize yourself moving forward to your next level.

_____

_____

_____

_____

As you close your eyes, picture the amazing day you will have tomorrow.

Tomorrow is a new day, filled with new opportunities.

Day 16 ◆ See how you are Multi-Faceted

Begin Each Day with Gratitude

10 things I am grateful for today…

1. _____

2. _____

3. _____

4. _____

5. _____

6. _____

7. _____

8. _____

9. _____

10. _____

Daily Action

Just as a diamond has many *facets* to the stone, so it is with our lives. We have many different angles we can see ourselves from and many different areas that make up who we are. In order to hold that "sparkle," we need to be fully engaged in each area of our lives.

What would I like the following *facets* of my life to look like in 5 years, 10 years, and 20 years?

1. Health

5 Years:	
10 Years:	
20 Years:	

2. Relationships

5 Years:	
10 Years:	
20 Years:	

3. Financial

5 Years:	
10 Years:	
20 Years:	

4. Business/Career/School

5 Years:	
10 Years:	
20 Years:	

5. Spiritual

5 Years:	
10 Years:	
20 Years:	

6. Recreation

5 Years:	
10 Years:	
20 Years:	

7. Community

5 Years:	
10 Years:	
20 Years:	

8. Personal Growth

5 Years:	
10 Years:	
20 Years:	

Daily Reflection

Before going to bed, review your gratitude list and reflect on your accomplishments and knowledge gained today. See the steps you've taken toward your future goals in all facets of your life. Acknowledge all the good in what you did today. Embrace it and move forward.

_____

_____

_____

_____

_____

As you close your eyes, picture the amazing day you will have tomorrow.

Tomorrow is a new day, filled with new opportunities.

Day 17 ◆ Create SMART Goals and Discover "The Why"

Begin Each Day with Gratitude

10 things I am grateful for today…

1. _____

2. _____

3. _____

4. _____

5. _____

6. _____

7. _____

8. _____

9. _____

10. _____

Daily Action

The following goals reflect what I want to see happen in the next year in each facet of my life. I will also consider WHY each goal is important to me and WHY I want to accomplish it.

Master List of Goals for _____ (year)

1. Health

Goal #1: _____

Why this Goal is important to me: _____

_____

Desired Date of Accomplishment: _____

Goal #2: _____

Why this Goal is important to me: _____

_____

Desired Date of Accomplishment: _____

2. Relationships

Goal #1: _____

Why this Goal is important to me: _____

_____

Desired Date of Accomplishment: _____

Goal #2: _____

Why this Goal is important to me: _____

_____

Desired Date of Accomplishment: _____

3. Financial

Goal #1: _____

Why this Goal is important to me: _____

_____

Desired Date of Accomplishment: _____

Goal #2: _____

Why this Goal is important to me: _____

_____

Desired Date of Accomplishment: _____

4. Business/Career/School

Goal #1: _____

Why this Goal is important to me: _____

_____

Desired Date of Accomplishment: _____

Goal #2: _____

Why this Goal is important to me: _____

_____

Desired Date of Accomplishment: _____

5. Spiritual

Goal #1: _____

Why this Goal is important to me: _____

_____

Desired Date of Accomplishment: _____

Goal #2: _____

Why this Goal is important to me: _____

_____

Desired Date of Accomplishment: _____

6. Recreation

Goal #1: _____

Why this Goal is important to me: _____

_____

Desired Date of Accomplishment: _____

Goal #2: _____

Why this Goal is important to me: _____

_____

Desired Date of Accomplishment: _____

7. Community

Goal #1: _____

Why this Goal is important to me: _____

_____

Desired Date of Accomplishment: _____

Goal #2: _____

Why this Goal is important to me: _____

_____

Desired Date of Accomplishment: _____

8. Personal Growth

Goal #1: _____

Why this Goal is important to me: _____

_____

Desired Date of Accomplishment: _____

Goal #2: _____

Why this Goal is important to me: _____

_____

Desired Date of Accomplishment: _____

Daily Reflection

Before going to bed, review your gratitude list and reflect on the day's accomplishments. Look for the good in what you did today. Embrace it and see yourself moving forward toward your SMART Goals. Your *Next Level of Living* is closer than you think!

_____

_____

_____

_____

_____

Your *Next Level of Living* is closer than you think! As you close your eyes, picture the amazing day you will have tomorrow.

Tomorrow is a new day, filled with new opportunities.

Day 18 ◆ Uncover the Five Power Questions

Begin Each Day with Gratitude

10 things I am grateful for today…

1. _____

2. _____

3. _____

4. _____

5. _____

6. _____

7. _____

8. _____

9. _____

10. _____

Daily Action

Asking myself the following questions will help me get clear about my priorities.

1. What personal needs do I have that, when fulfilled, will make me a happier and better person?

_____

_____

_____

2. What have I always wanted to do but have been afraid to attempt?

_____

_____

3. What do I enjoy doing most in my life, and if money was no object I would do full time?

_____

_____

_____

4. When I have reached the end of my life, what do I want to look back and feel good about? What do I want to be remembered for?

_____

_____

_____

5. If I only had six months to live, how would I spend my time? Where would I go? What would I do? Who would I want to spend time with?

_____

_____

_____

Daily Reflection

Before going to bed, review your gratitude list and reflect on the day's accomplishments. Know that even after you go to sleep tonight, your brain will continue to seek answers to the questions you put into play today. Embrace this forward progress and celebrate where you are on your journey to the next level.

_____

_____

_____

As you close your eyes, picture the amazing day you will have tomorrow.

Tomorrow is a new day, filled with new opportunities.

Day 19 ◆ Set Your Top 6 Goals

Begin Each Day with Gratitude

10 things I am grateful for today…

1. _____

2. _____

3. _____

4. _____

5. _____

6. _____

7. _____

8. _____

9. _____

10. _____

Daily Action

I will now pare down my Master List of Goals *(from Day 17)* to my Top 6 Goals. In order for these goals to be achieved, I know my thoughts and actions need to be focused on them. If for some reason I was only able to accomplish 6 goals, these would be the most important to me. They are the goals that I REALLY want to accomplish.

My Top 6 Goals are:

1. _____

2. _____

3. _____

4. _____

5. _____

6. _____

Daily Reflection

Before going to bed, review your gratitude list and reflect on the day's accomplishments. Even as you read this, those accomplishments are moving you one step closer toward your goals. Look for the good in what you did today. Embrace it and move forward.

_____

_____

_____

_____

_____

_____

_____

As you close your eyes, picture the amazing day you will have tomorrow.

Tomorrow is a new day, filled with new opportunities.

Day 20 ◆ Determine Where the Rubber Meets the Road

Begin Each Day with Gratitude

10 things I am grateful for today…

1. _____
2. _____
3. _____
4. _____
5. _____
6. _____
7. _____
8. _____
9. _____
10. _____

Daily Action

For each goal on my Top 6 Goals List from yesterday, these are the action steps I must take to accomplish each one. Getting clear about all the actions needed will give me a game plan to achieve my goals.

Goal #1: _____

Desired Date of Accomplishment for this Goal: _____

What action steps will I take to achieve this goal?

    Step 1: _____

    Step 2: _____

    Step 3: _____

(Add as many more steps as you need to reach your goal)

_____

_____

_____

_____

Goal #2: _____

Desired Date of Accomplishment for this Goal: _____

What action steps will I take to achieve this goal?

    Step 1: _____

    Step 2: _____

    Step 3: _____

(Add as many more steps as you need to reach your goal)

_____

_____

_____

_____

SECTION TWO ◆ Day 20

Goal #3: _____

Desired Date of Accomplishment for this Goal: _____

What action steps will I take to achieve this goal?

    Step 1: _____

    Step 2: _____

    Step 3: _____

(Add as many more steps as you need to reach your goal)

_____

_____

_____

_____

Goal #4: _____

Desired Date of Accomplishment for this Goal: _____

What action steps will I take to achieve this goal?

    Step 1: _____

    Step 2: _____

    Step 3: _____

(Add as many more steps as you need to reach your goal)

_____

_____

_____

_____

Goal #5: _____

Desired Date of Accomplishment for this Goal: _____

What action steps will I take to achieve this goal?

Step 1: _____

Step 2: _____

Step 3: _____

(Add as many more steps as you need to reach your goal)

_____

_____

_____

_____

Goal #6: _____

Desired Date of Accomplishment for this Goal: _____

What action steps will I take to achieve this goal?

Step 1: _____

Step 2: _____

Step 3: _____

(Add as many more steps as you need to reach your goal)

_____

_____

_____

_____

Daily Reflection

Before going to bed, review your gratitude list and reflect on the action you took today. Look for the good, celebrate it and continue moving forward on your journey.

_____

_____

_____

_____

_____

_____

_____

_____

_____

_____

_____

_____

_____

_____

_____

As you close your eyes, picture the amazing day you will have tomorrow.

Tomorrow is a new day, filled with new opportunities.

Day 21 ◆ Seek Feedback and Evaluations

Begin Each Day with Gratitude

10 things I am grateful for today…

1. _____

2. _____

3. _____

4. _____

5. _____

6. _____

7. _____

8. _____

9. _____

10. _____

Daily Action

The following are three people I will share my goals with and allow them to support me during my *Next Level Living* journey. My list of support beams on Day 6 can also provide me with some possible people to choose from.

Person's Name	When and How Will I Share My Goals With Them?

How often will I evaluate my progress?

_____

My first evaluation is going to be on (date): _____.

During each evaluation I will ask myself and discuss with those supporting me:
- What is working?
- What is not working?
- What changes are needed to get better results?

Daily Reflection

Before going to bed, reflect on the day's accomplishments. Look for the good in them, embrace them and move forward.

_____

_____

_____

_____

_____

_____

_____

_____

As you close your eyes, picture the amazing day you will have tomorrow.

Tomorrow is a new day, filled with new opportunities.

Day 22 ◆ Stick to Your Plan

Begin Each Day with Gratitude

10 things I am grateful for today…

1. _____

2. _____

3. _____

4. _____

5. _____

6. _____

7. _____

8. _____

9. _____

10. _____

Daily Action

Things that help me "KEEP going."

1. _____

2. _____

3. _____

Things that help me "GET going again" when I feel stuck.

1. _____

2. _____

3. _____

Daily Reflection

Before going to bed, reflect on your accomplishments today. Look for the collective good, embrace it and move forward.

_____

_____

_____

_____

_____

_____

_____

_____

_____

_____

_____

_____

_____

_____

As you close your eyes, picture the amazing day you will have tomorrow.

Tomorrow is a new day, filled with new opportunities.

SECTION THREE:

Support Your Journey with Affirmations & Visualization

Day 23 ◆ Write Affirmations that Create Action

Begin Each Day with Gratitude

10 things I am grateful for today…

1. _____

2. _____

3. _____

4. _____

5. _____

6. _____

7. _____

8. _____

9. _____

10. _____

Daily Action

In order to create valuable positive affirmations, use the following language:

1. **The present tense.** The words "I am" are the most powerful words in creating effective affirmations. Your affirmation should describe what you want as though you already have it or as though you have accomplished the goal.

2. **Positive statements.** It is important to be very clear on what you want rather than focusing on what you don't want. If we focus on what we don't want, that's what we get.

3. **Short and specific statements.** Your affirmation must be short enough to be easily memorized and use very specific rather than general wording.

4. **Personal Power.** Your affirmations should not get tangled up with what others expect from you or what you expect from them. They are all about you and you alone.

5. **Open Ended and Limitless.** When you become clear and specific on what you desire, add the words "or something better" to your affirmations.

Today's Date:

Using your Top 6 Goals, create an affirmation for each of them *(for examples of affirmations refer to the Appendix section of your book).*

Goal #1:

Affirmation:

_____

_____

Goal #2:

Affirmation:

_____

_____

Goal #3:

Affirmation:

_____

_____

Goal #4:

Affirmation:

_____

_____

Goal #5:

Affirmation:

_____

_____

Goal #6:

Affirmation:

_____

_____

The type of affirmations you just wrote are directly associated with a specific goal. The second type of affirmation is called a _Connector Affirmation_. This type of affirmation helps position your thinking and helps you connect to certain emotions and mindsets.

Now, create as many Connector Affirmations as you want _(for examples refer to the Appendix section of your book)_:

_____

_____

_____

_____

_____

_____

_____

_____

Daily Reflection

Before going to bed, review your gratitude list and reflect on the day's accomplishments. Look for the good in what you did and celebrate the powerful affirmations that you put into words today. Embrace your success and continue moving forward toward your next level.

_____

_____

_____

_____

_____

_____

_____

_____

_____

_____

_____

As you close your eyes, picture the amazing day you will have tomorrow.

Tomorrow is a new day, filled with new opportunities.

Day 24 ◆ Bring Life to Your Goals

Begin Each Day with Gratitude

10 things I am grateful for today…

1. _____

2. _____

3. _____

4. _____

5. _____

6. _____

7. _____

8. _____

9. _____

10. _____

Daily Action

Today is the day to start creating your own vision board! After reviewing your Top 6 Goals, Master List of Goals, and your BE, DO and HAVE lists, collect pictures that relate to these goals.

While you are scanning through magazines or print material, pay close attention to words, colors or diagrams that connect with you. Don't think too long about whether you should have them on your board or not. If your eye is drawn to it, grab it and save it. Just focus on gathering a collection of visuals for your board. Once you start placing them on the board, only then will you decide what to keep and what to toss. For now, simply collect pictures with the intention of creating a collection of visuals that evoke a pleasant emotion and that you enjoy looking at.

Daily Reflection

Before going to bed, review your gratitude list and reflect on the day's accomplishments. Look for the good in what you did today and reflect on the excitement of bringing your goals to life with a vision board. Embrace this excitement and move forward in your journey.

_____

_____

_____

_____

_____

_____

_____

_____

_____

_____

_____

As you close your eyes, picture the amazing day you will have tomorrow.

Tomorrow is a new day, filled with new opportunities.

Day 25 ◆ Explore Different Types of Vision Boards

Begin Each Day with Gratitude

10 things I am grateful for today…

1. _____

2. _____

3. _____

4. _____

5. _____

6. _____

7. _____

8. _____

9. _____

10. _____

Daily Action

Now choose the type of vision board or vision book you would like to create:

☐ Business   ☐ Whole Life   ☐ Specific Facet/Goal

☐ Open and Allowing   ☐ Annual   ☐ Transition

Continue to collect the remaining materials needed:

- more magazines
- scissors
- glue stick
- poster board or heavy bond paper
- hole punch if you are making a vision book using a three ring binder

Set aside time over the next few days to work on this project.

Daily Reflection

Before going to bed, review your gratitude list and reflect on what you accomplished today. See how your vision of life at the next level is steadily becoming a reality. Embrace what is and move forward to what will soon be.

_____

_____

_____

_____

_____

_____

_____

_____

_____

_____

_____

_____

_____

_____

As you close your eyes, picture the amazing day you will have tomorrow.

Tomorrow is a new day, filled with new opportunities.

Day 26 ◆ Keep Pressing On

Begin Each Day with Gratitude

10 <u>courageous things about myself</u> I am grateful for today...

1. _____

2. _____

3. _____

4. _____

5. _____

6. _____

7. _____

8. _____

9. _____

10. _____

Daily Action

Go back and review the work you have done up to this point. Remember where you are heading and why you are heading there. Spend a few minutes today reading through your Top 6 Goals and then continue working on your vision board until it is complete.

Daily Reflection

Before going to bed, review your list of list of courageous things about yourself and reflect on how they contributed to the day's accomplishments. Celebrate the results you noticed today. Whether you consider the results big or small, they are all victories. Embrace the feeling of winning and move forward.

_____

_____

_____

_____

_____

_____

_____

_____

_____

_____

_____

_____

_____

_____

As you close your eyes, picture the amazing day you will have tomorrow, leaping tall buildings in a single bound!

Tomorrow is a new day, filled with new opportunities.

Day 27 ◆ Be Persistently Perseverant

Begin Each Day with Gratitude

10 things I am grateful for today…

1. _____

2. _____

3. _____

4. _____

5. _____

6. _____

7. _____

8. _____

9. _____

10. _____

Daily Action

To ensure your success in achieving your dreams and goals, make a decision now about how you will master the art of **persistence** and **perseverance**.

Describe what you will do and who you will need around you to help you be **persistent** in reaching your goals.

_____

_____

_____

_____

Daily Reflection

Before going to bed, review your gratitude list and reflect on the day's accomplishments. Look for the good in what you did today. Embrace your ability to exercise persistence and move forward toward your next level.

_____

_____

_____

_____

_____

_____

_____

_____

_____

_____

_____

_____

_____

_____

As you close your eyes, picture the amazing day you will have tomorrow.

Tomorrow is a new day, filled with new opportunities.

Day 28 ◆ Gain Satisfaction

Begin Each Day with Gratitude

10 things I am grateful for <u>in this moment</u>…

1. _____

2. _____

3. _____

4. _____

5. _____

6. _____

7. _____

8. _____

9. _____

10. _____

Daily Action

Three things I have learned about myself from going through the *Next Level Living* process up to this day:

1. _____

2. _____

3. _____

What has been difficult?

_____

_____

_____

Why was it difficult?

_____

_____

What has been beneficial?

_____

_____

Why was it beneficial?

_____

_____

What has been motivating?

_____

_____

Why was it motivating?

_____

_____

Daily Reflection

Before going to bed, review your gratitude list and reflect on the day's accomplishments. Look for the good in what you did today and the progress you've made so far. Embrace what you are feeling in this moment before moving forward in your journey.

_____

_____

_____

As you close your eyes, picture the amazing day you will have tomorrow.

Tomorrow is a new day, filled with new opportunities.

Day 29 ◆ Reach for your Rope of Hope

Begin Each Day with Gratitude

10 things I am grateful for today…

1. _____
2. _____
3. _____
4. _____
5. _____
6. _____
7. _____
8. _____
9. _____
10. _____

Daily Action

Who or what would you consider to be your **rope(s) of hope**? These are the stronghold(s) that will carry you through all types of challenges.

1. _____
2. _____
3. _____
4. _____
5. _____
6. _____

7. _____

8. _____

9. _____

10. _____

Daily Reflection

Before going to bed, review your gratitude list and reflect on the day's accomplishments. As you move into the last leg of your journey, look for examples of how the people who love or care about you have been supporting you the whole time. See the good in what you did today. Embrace it and move forward.

_____

_____

_____

_____

_____

_____

_____

_____

_____

As you close your eyes, picture the amazing day you will have tomorrow.

Tomorrow is a new day, filled with new opportunities.

SECTION FOUR:

Celebrate Your Journey

Day 30 ◆ Complete the Climb with Celebration

Begin Each Day with Gratitude

10 things to celebrate I am grateful for today…

1. _____

2. _____

3. _____

4. _____

5. _____

6. _____

7. _____

8. _____

9. _____

10. _____

Daily Action

Take some time to consider your accomplishments to date. I am certain you can easily find numerous things to celebrate. You've made it to the final section of the *Next Level Living* process by doing your exercises and growing over the last 30 days. I would say this calls for a fist pump or victory dance — doesn't it?

_____

_____

_____

_____

_____

_____

_____

_____

_____

_____

Daily Reflection

Before going to bed, review your gratitude list and reflect on your personal celebrations of the day. Acknowledge the good in what you did today, embrace it and move forward. You are closer to your next level than ever before!

_____

_____

_____

_____

_____

_____

_____

_____

_____

As you close your eyes, picture the amazing day you will have tomorrow.

Tomorrow is a new day, filled with new opportunities.

Day 31 ◆ Discover the Difference between Happiness and Joy

Begin Each Day with Gratitude

10 things I am grateful for today…

1. _____

2. _____

3. _____

4. _____

5. _____

6. _____

7. _____

8. _____

9. _____

10. _____

Daily Action

Specific things that make me **HAPPY:**

1. _____

2. _____

3. _____

4. _____

5. _____

6. _____

7. _____

8. _____

9. _____

10. _____

Specific ways I connect with **JOY** in my life:

1. _____

2. _____

3. _____

4. _____

5. _____

6. _____

7. _____

8. _____

9. _____

10. _____

Daily Reflection

Before going to bed, review your gratitude list and reflect on the day's accomplishments. Look for the happiness and joy you found throughout the day. Embrace this and move forward in your journey to the next level.

_____

_____

_____

As you close your eyes, picture the amazing day you will have tomorrow.

Tomorrow is a new day, filled with new opportunities.

Day 32 ◆ Celebrate YOU

Begin Each Day with Gratitude

10 things I am grateful for today…

1. _____
2. _____
3. _____
4. _____
5. _____
6. _____
7. _____
8. _____
9. _____
10. _____

Daily Action

Make a list of how you would like to celebrate and with whom (if anyone) you will do this celebrating. Get it on your calendar and don't let the busyness of life take over.

1. _____
2. _____
3. _____
4. _____
5. _____
6. _____

7. _____

8. _____

9. _____

10. _____

Daily Reflection

Before going to bed, review all your gratitude lists from your journey and reflect on all the incredible accomplishments of your *Next Level Living* journey. Look for the good in what you did today and for the past 32 days. Embrace it ALL and continue moving forward!

_____

_____

_____

_____

_____

_____

_____

_____

As always, as you close your eyes, picture the amazing day you will have tomorrow and all the days beyond. The journey never ends and your available levels are infinite!

Tomorrow is a new day, filled with new opportunities.

Your Journey Continues

Congratulations on your success in completing your first 32 days of *Next Level Living*. I hope your journey so far has been full of inspiration, discovery, and learning, and that along the way you picked up a treasure chest of jewels and tools to enhance and ensure your continued success.

Now is the time to recommit and continue on the journey toward another level. Keep up the momentum by frequently revisiting what you have written here in the workbook and by putting what you have learned into daily practice. As you continue moving forward, here are the ideal, most productive next steps you can take.

Every Day:

- ◆ Practice Gratitude
- ◆ Think strong, positive thoughts
- ◆ Look at your vision board/note cards
- ◆ Ensure that your actions are moving you in the direction of your goals

Monthly:

- ◆ Review every facet of your life
- ◆ Pay attention to your goal date(s)
- ◆ Evaluate your progress and make adjustments if necessary

Annually:

- ◆ Go through the *Next Level Living* process for the 8 facets of your life
- ◆ Create a Master List of Goals
- ◆ Create your Top 6 Goals
- ◆ Create affirmations to support your goals
- ◆ Create a new vision board

Remember, there are infinite levels of living available to you, but you must keep climbing. Nobody can walk up to the next level for you. Consider the material you have learned here as a flashlight to light your way.

This is not the end of your journey… It's just the beginning!

Notes

Notes

Notes